Busy Ant Maths

Activity Book 1C

Name game

Date: ______________________

Read and write numbers from 1 to 20 in numerals and words

Teacher's notes

Children read each number written on the T-shirts and write the same number in numerals into the space.

Plaice value

Date: ____________________

Recognise place value in numbers to 20

You will need:
- coloured pencils

Teacher's notes

Children colour one portion of fish and one portion of chips to match the shirt of the customer buying them.

Counting sets of more than 20

Date: ____________________

Practise counting sets of more than 20

You will need:
- orange and green coloured pencils

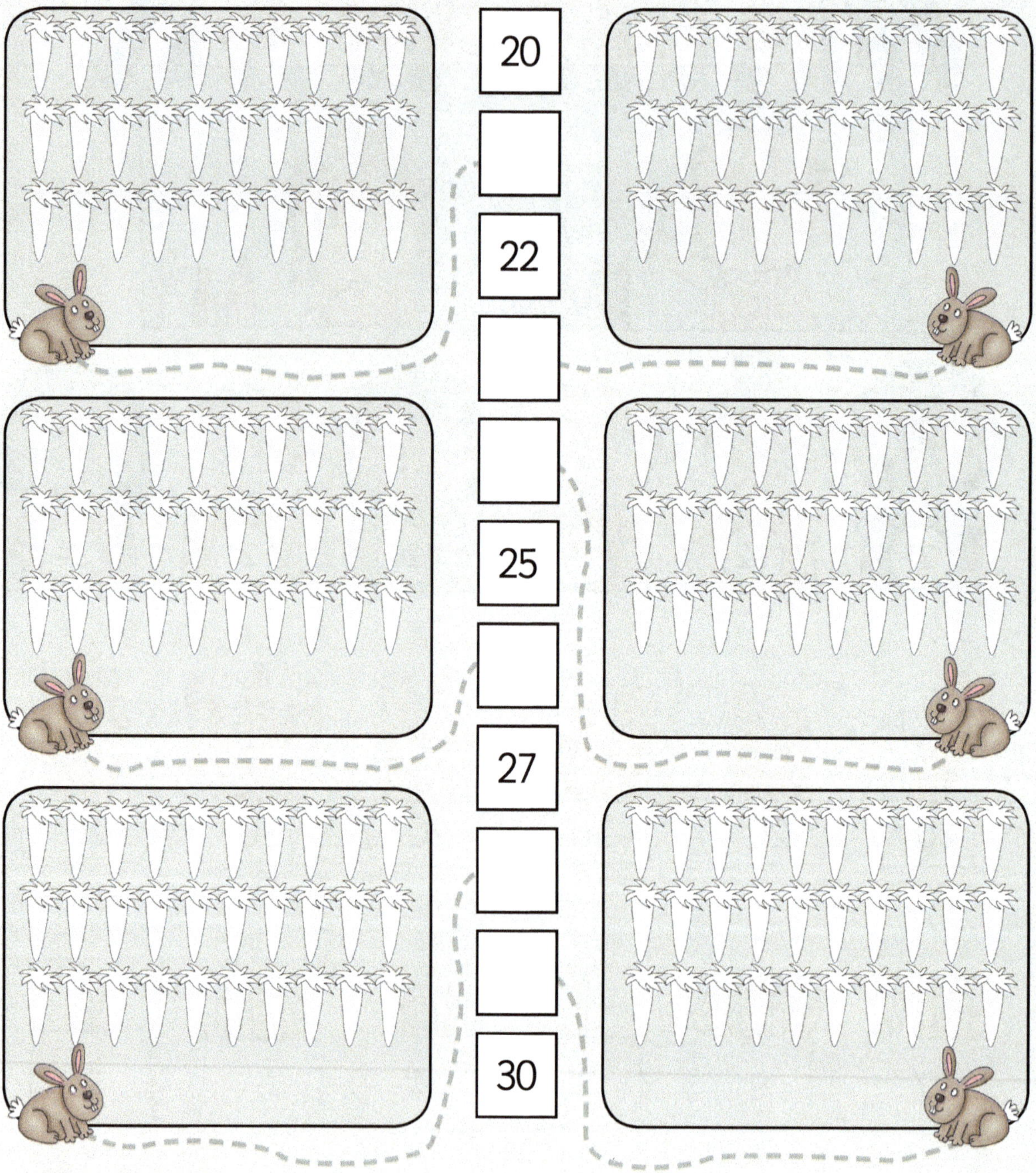

Teacher's notes

Children complete the number track from 20 to 30, writing the missing numbers into the spaces. They then follow each rabbit's track, to find out how many carrots they need to count and colour in that field.

Date: ____________________

Counting machines

Count on or back in 2s, 5s and 10s

1 | 3 | ___ | ___ | 9 | ___ | ___ | ___

6 | 11 | 16 | ___ | ___ | 31 | 36 | ___

37 | ___ | 57 | 67 | ___ | ___ | ___ | ___

19 | 17 | ___ | ___ | 11 | ___ | ___ | ___

51 | 46 | ___ | ___ | 31 | ___ | 21 | ___

94 | 84 | ___ | ___ | 54 | ___ | ___ | 24

Teacher's notes

Children complete the sequence for each counting machine by counting on or back in 2s, 5s or 10s. They then write the missing numbers in the spaces provided.

At the double!

Date: ___________________

Know doubles of all numbers from 1 to 10

You will need:
- coloured pencils

Teacher's notes

In each section, children look at the numbers on each pair of runners' tops and work out the addition double. They then find the finishing flag showing the answer to each pair and colour both tops to match.

Date: ____________________

Longship addition

Use doubles to help solve addition problems

Teacher's notes

Children solve the addition calculation on each Viking longship, using an addition double to help them. They then continue the line from each ship to show the route to the addition double island that helped to solve the problem.

Date: ____________________

Penguin problems

Solve number problems

□ + □ + □ = 15

□ + □ + □ = 17

□ + □ + □ = 15

□ + □ + □ = 17

□ + □ + □ = 16

□ + □ + □ = 18

□ + □ + □ = 16

□ + □ + □ = 18

Teacher's notes

For each question, children write three numbers which, when added together, make 15, 16, 17 or 18. They can use the penguin number track to help them.

Date: ______________

Talented trios

Recall addition and subtraction facts to 20 and use them to work out other facts

You will need:
- paper

☐ + ☐ = ☐

☐ – ☐ = ☐

☐ + ☐ = ☐

☐ – ☐ = ☐

☐ + ☐ = ☐

☐ – ☐ = ☐

☐ + ☐ = ☐

☐ – ☐ = ☐

Teacher's notes

Children look at the numbers on each musical trio and write one addition and one subtraction fact using the three numbers. They then find the other two facts for each trio, writing the answers on a sheet of paper.

Date: ________________

Where is Toby?

Use position words

Toby is…

__________ the box.

__________ the tree.

__________ the hill.

__________ the tent.

__________ the wall.

__________ the clock.

on top of	underneath	in front of	behind	inside	outside

Teacher's notes

Children look at each picture to decide where Toby is. They then use the words and phrases at the bottom of the page to complete the sentences.

Date: ____________________

Where on the farm?

Understand position words

You will need:
- coloured pencils

Draw:

 near to .

 far from .

 around .

 close to .

 and 

 and 

 and 

far

near

around

Teacher's notes

Children follow the instructions to draw animals and objects in correct positions on the farm. They then identify pairs of objects on the farm and draw a line to the best position word for each pair.

Hungry insects

Date: ____________________

Understand and use direction words

forwards
left ← ↑ ↓ → right
backwards

left ←

backwards ↓

forwards ↑

right →

	right →	backwards ↓

Teacher's notes

In the top section, children follow the directions for each insect from one leaf to another. They then draw a line to match each insect to the fruit it eats. In the bottom section, children draw a circle around the one uneaten fruit from the first exercise. They then use two words and/or two arrows to write instructions for each insect to reach the uneaten fruit.

Date: ____________________

View from a hill

Recognise and make whole, half, quarter and three-quarter turns

You will need:
- coloured pencils

sees	turns	sees
	quarter	
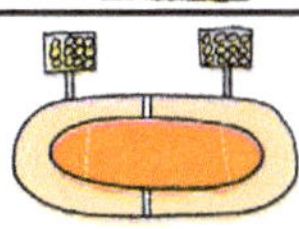		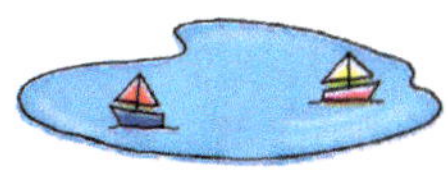
	three-quarter	
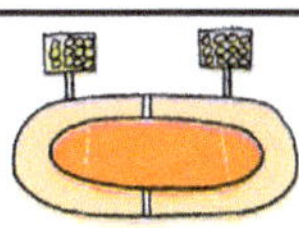		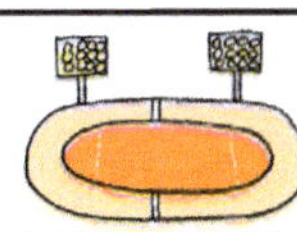
	half	

Teacher's notes

Children draw what the person on the hill will see when they make a turn to the right (clockwise), or write how far the person on the hill needs to turn to the right (clockwise) to see the second feature.

Date: ____________

Kangaroo 2s

Count in multiples of 2

0	2			8
10	8		4	
10		14		
20	18			
22		26		30
28	26			

Teacher's notes

In each row, children count on or back in 2s and write the missing numbers in the spaces.

Date: ____________

Count sets of 2

Make connections between arrays, number patterns and counting in 2s

You will need:
- coloured pencils

4 lots of 2

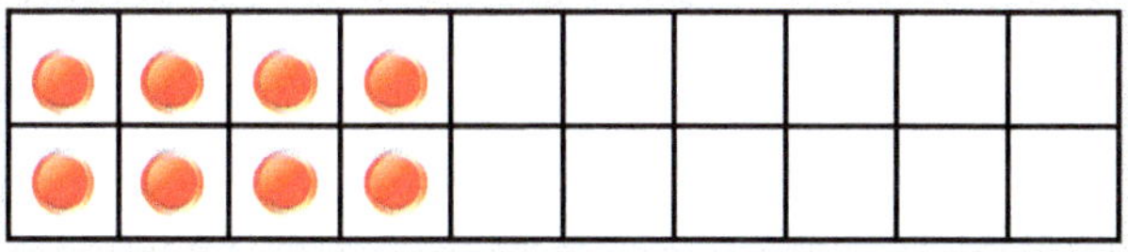

make ☐ altogether.

9 lots of 2

make ☐ altogether.

5 lots of 2

make ☐ altogether.

8 lots of 2

make ☐ altogether.

6 lots of 2

make ☐ altogether.

10 lots of 2

make ☐ altogether.

Teacher's notes

Children follow the instructions to draw and colour an array of counters in each section. They write the total number of counters in each array in the space provided.

Date: ____________________

Quilt counting

Count in multiples of 5 and 10

0	5			20
45	40		30	
30		40		50
0	10		30	
70	60			30
60				100

Teacher's notes

In each row of the patchwork quilt, children count on or back in 5s or 10s and write the missing numbers in the spaces.

Date: ________________

Apple arrays

Make connections between arrays, number patterns and counting in 5s and 10s

You will need:
- red or green coloured pencils

Show an array of 10.

Show an array of 15.

Show an array of 16.

Show an array of 20.

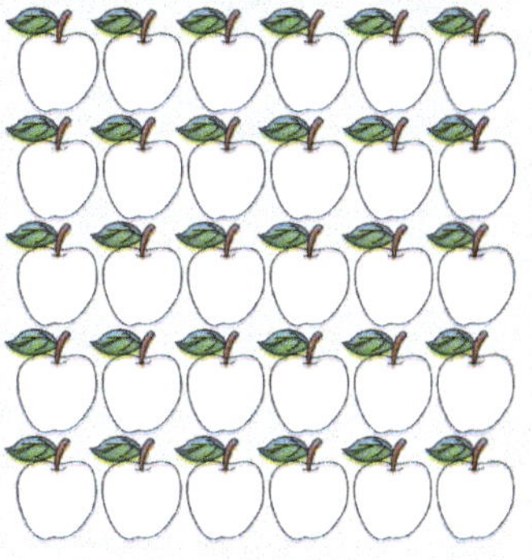

Show an array of 25.

Show an array of 30.

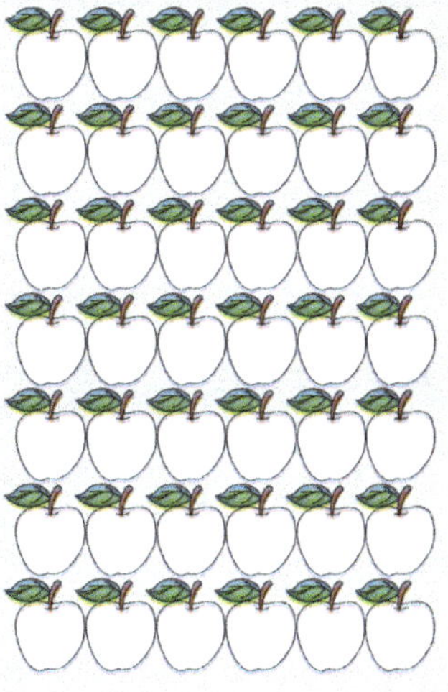

Teacher's notes

Children colour the apples in red or green to show the arrays in each section.

Sweet shop sets

Date: ___________________

Count sets of 2, 5 or 10 to find a total

		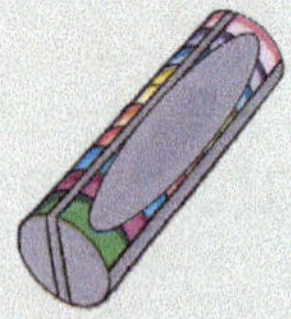
2 sweets	5 sweets	10 sweets

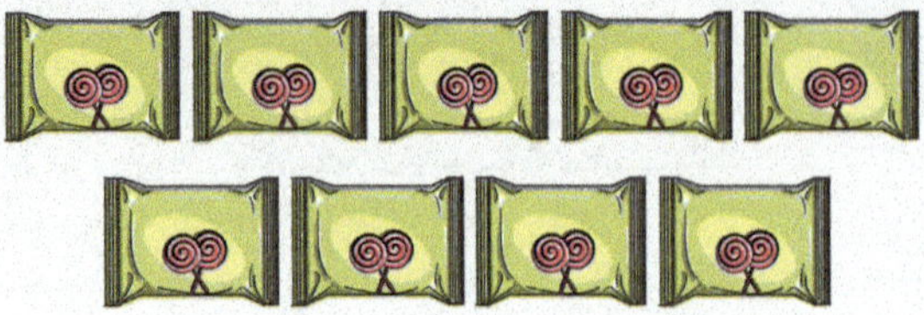

☐ packets

☐ sweets altogether

☐ packets

☐ sweets altogether

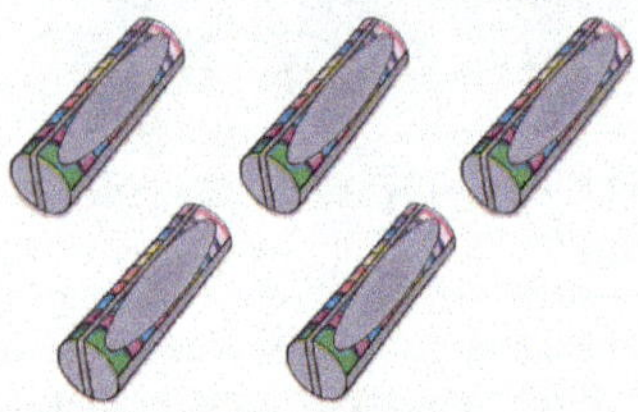

☐ packets

☐ sweets altogether

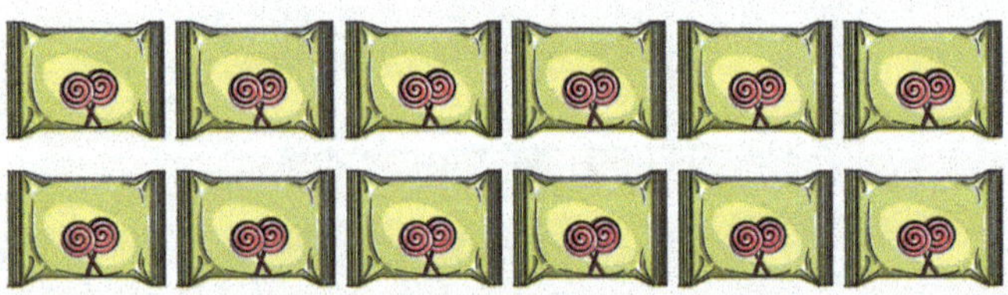

☐ packets

☐ sweets altogether

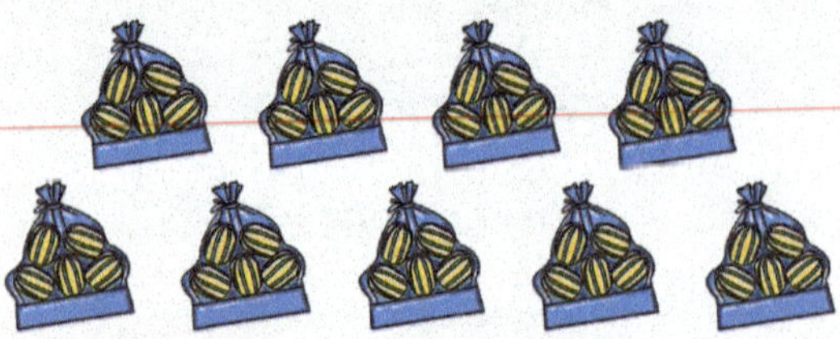

☐ packets

☐ sweets altogether

Teacher's notes

For each set of sweets, children count and write down how many packets there are. They then count in 2s, 5s or 10s to find out how many sweets there are altogether in each set.

Date: ____________

Solving shopping problems

Count sets of 2, 5 or 10 to solve problems

There are 2 socks in each pair. There are 8 pairs.

There are ☐ socks altogether.

There are 5 pens in each pot. There are 6 pots.

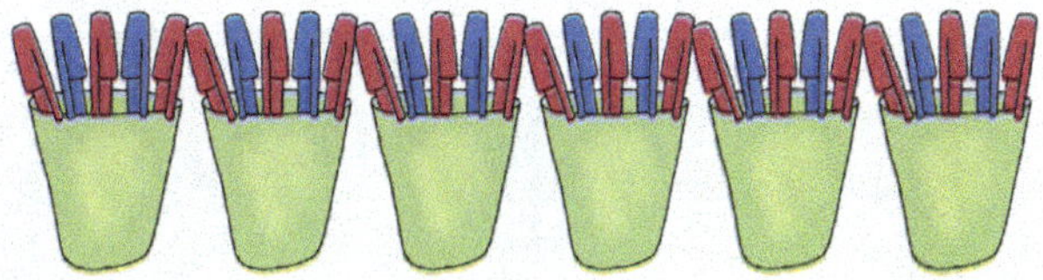

There are ☐ pens altogether.

There are 10 sweets in 1 bag. There are 7 bags.

There are ☐ sweets altogether.

Sam has collected 2c coins. He has 9 coins.

Sam has ☐c altogether.

Halle has 5 books on each shelf. She has 7 shelves.

Halle has ☐ books altogether.

Ellis has 10 stickers on each page. There are 9 pages altogether.

Ellis has ☐ stickers altogether.

Teacher's notes

Children read each problem and complete them by counting in sets of 2, 5 or 10.

Date: ____________

Cookie shares

Share objects into equal groups

☐ shared between ☐ is ☐.

☐ shared between ☐ is ☐.

☐ shared between ☐ is ☐.

☐ shared between ☐ is ☐.

Teacher's notes

Children count the number of cookies in the set, then share them equally between the trays by drawing them onto each one. Then, they complete the sentence underneath.

Date: ______________

Fair shares

Solve problems involving sharing

Toffee apples

☐ toffee apples shared between ☐ makes ☐ each.

Dodgems

☐ children sitting in ☐ dodgems is ☐ in each.

Helter skelter

Ella buys 14 tickets. She shares them between 7.

☐ shared between ☐ is ☐.

Cups and saucers

☐ children sitting in ☐ cups and saucers is ☐ in each cup.

Candy floss

☐ candy flosses shared between ☐ makes ☐ each.

Carousel

Leon buys 4 tickets and spends 20c. How much is 1 ticket? ☐ shared between ☐ is ☐c.

Teacher's notes

Children read each problem and solve it by writing the correct numbers and answers into the boxes underneath.

The ruler and the metre rule

Date: ____________

Measure using a ruler and understand what a metre rule is

You will need:
- ruler
- metre rule

Shorter than a ruler	Longer than a ruler

Shorter than a metre	Longer or taller than a metre

Teacher's notes

At the top of the page children draw pictures of two objects that are shorter and two objects that are longer than a 30 centimetre ruler. They then measure the real objects and write the lengths underneath their drawings. At the bottom of the page children draw pictures of objects that are shorter and longer or taller than a metre rule.

Estimating and measuring

Date: ____________________

Estimate and measure lengths and heights

You will need:
- ruler
- metre rule
- glue stick
- book
- scissors
- small bottle
- chair

Object	Estimate	Measurement

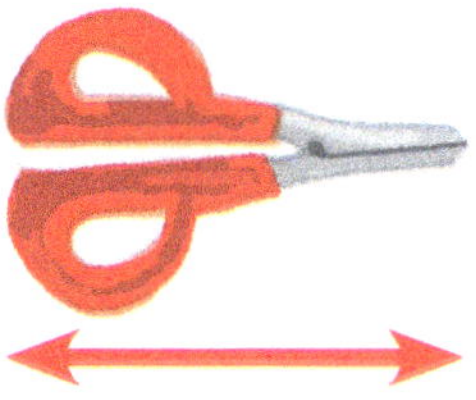		
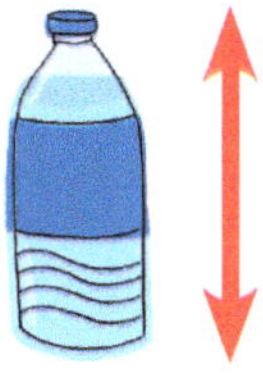		

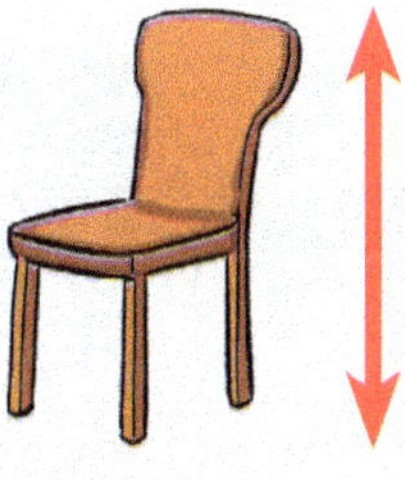

Teacher's notes

Children estimate the length or height of each real object. They then use a 30 centimetre ruler to measure the actual length/height. They write their estimates and measurements in the appropriate spaces in the table. Then children use a metre rule to measure the height of a chair.

Date: ____________________

How many bricks?

Solve problems about mass

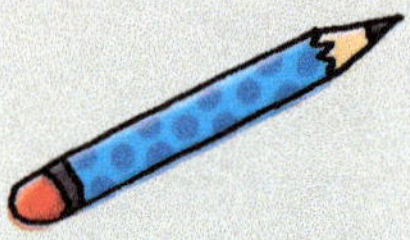
2 blocks

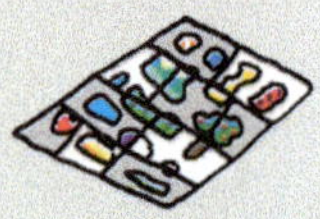
5 blocks

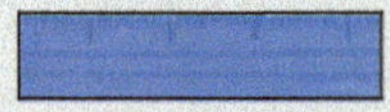
1 block

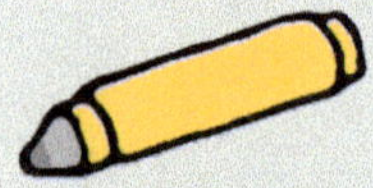
3 blocks

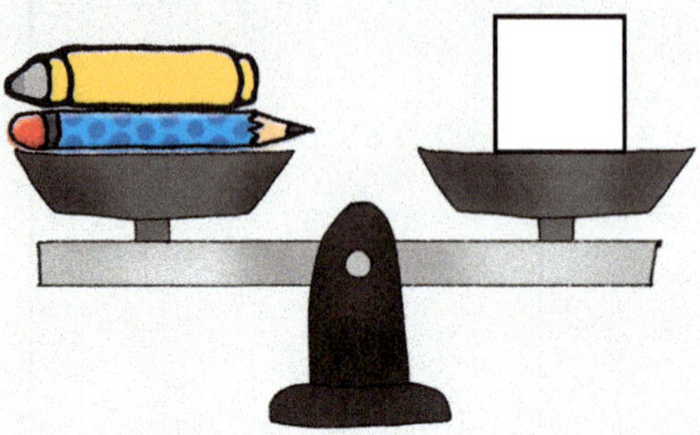

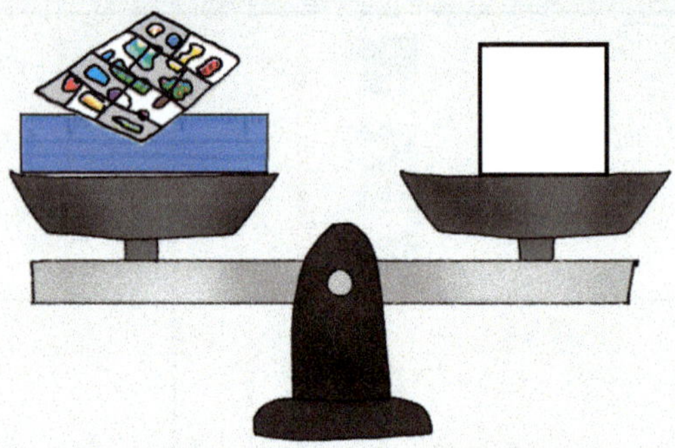

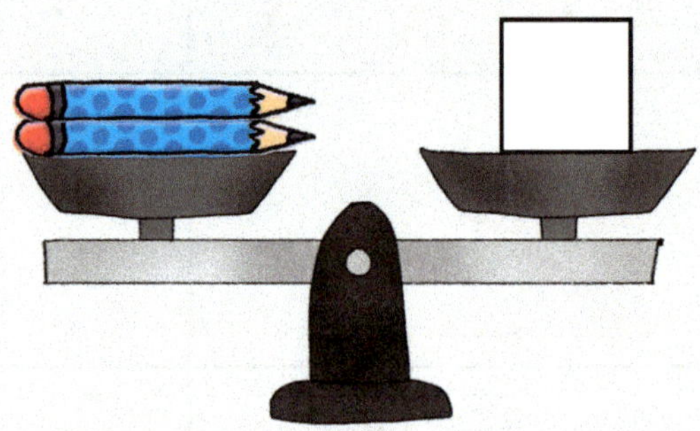

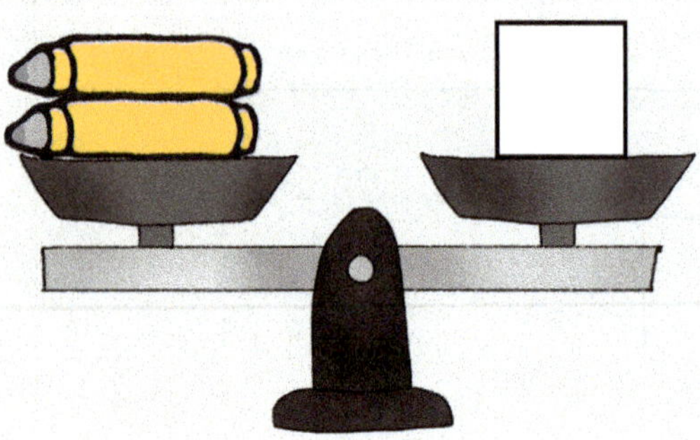

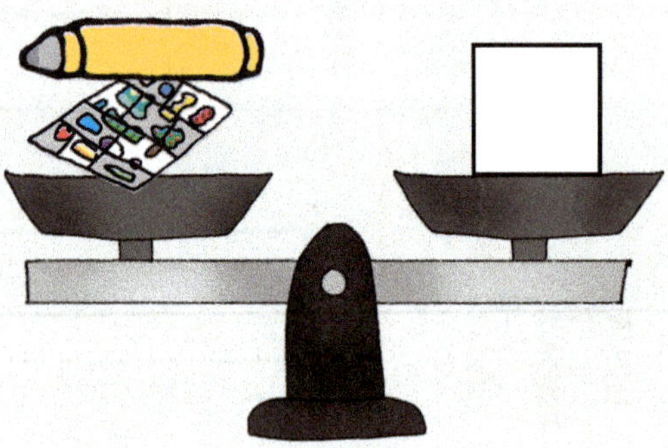

Teacher's notes

Children work out the different weight combinations of each pair of objects then write the number of blocks that are needed to make it balance.

Date: ____________________

Shapes that balance

Solve problems about mass

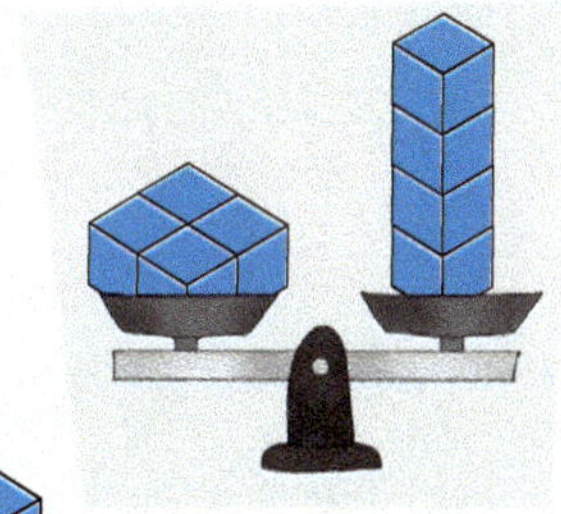

Teacher's notes

Children draw lines to show shapes that would balance on a pan balance.

Date: ____________

Monkey mix-up

Know addition and subtraction facts to 20

$11 + 3 =$	$15 - 7 =$
$12 - 2 =$	$9 + 8 =$
$14 + 1 =$	$18 - 9 =$
$13 - 0 =$	$11 + 5 =$
$12 + 4 =$	$20 - 13 =$
$14 - 3 =$	$7 + 11 =$
$16 + 4 =$	$19 - 0 =$

Teacher's notes

Children look at each addition or subtraction calculation in turn and write the correct answer in the box. They can use the 0–20 number track to support their working out.

Date: ____________________

Train patterns

Recognise patterns in addition and subtraction

$10 + 5 = \square$ $\quad 11 + \square = 15$ $\quad \square + 3 = 15$

$16 - 6 = \square$ $\quad 16 - \square = 9$ $\quad 16 - 8 = \square$

$9 + 8 = \square$ $\quad 10 + \square = 17$ $\quad 11 + \square = 17$

$19 - 7 = \square$ $\quad 19 - 8 = \square$ $\quad 19 - \square = 10$

$17 + 3 = \square$ $\quad 16 + \square = 20$ $\quad \square + 5 = 20$

Teacher's notes

Children complete the addition or subtraction pattern shown on each set of engine and carriages, writing the correct numbers into the boxes.

Fairground problems

Date: ______________

Solve word problems

9 people were on the dodgems. 7 people joined them.

How many people were on the dodgems altogether?

18 people were on the rollercoaster. Ella, Min, Amir and Cal got off.

How many people were left on the rollercoaster?

There were 20 toffee apples. Emma bought 2 of them.

How many toffee apples were left?

There were 12 prizes on the top shelf and 8 more on the bottom shelf.

How many prizes were there altogether?

Teacher's notes

Children read each word problem. They then write the addition or subtraction calculation in the boxes.

Date: ____________

Add and takeaway menu

Solve problems involving money

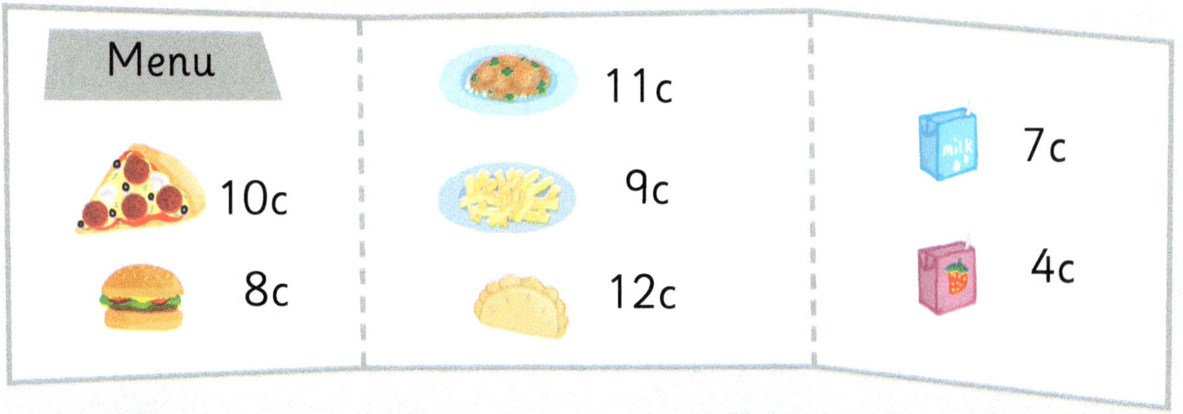

Hattie spends:

Her change is:

Yuko spends:

Her change is:

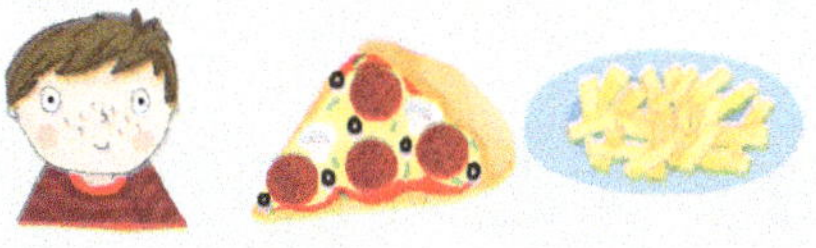

Caie spends:

His change is:

Cavan spends:

His change is:

Teacher's notes

Children look at the menu. Each child has 20c to spend. They first work out how much each child spends and then calculate the change they each receive.

Date: ____________________

Yoyo spending

Know addition and subtraction facts to 20

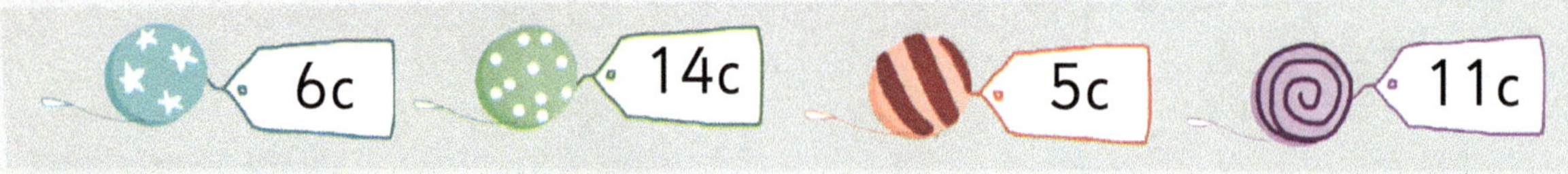

Naomi buys:

Naomi spends:

☐ c

Amir buys:

Amir spends:

☐ c

Lucy buys:

Lucy spends:

☐ c

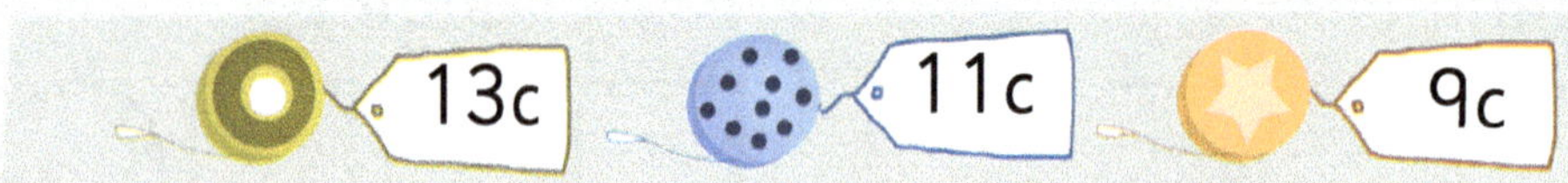

Lucas has 19c.

He buys:

Lucas has ☐ c change.

Ava has 18c.

She buys:

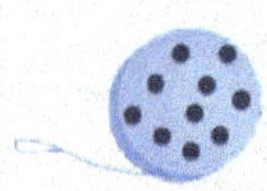

Ava has ☐ c change.

Isaac has 20c.

He buys:

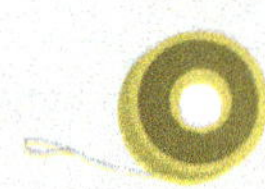

Isaac has ☐ c change.

Teacher's notes

Children look at each addition or subtraction problem in turn and use the space underneath to work out each one, writing the answer in the box.

Date: ____________________

Money Lane

Solve problems involving money

Thea had 18c.
Her change was 8c.

[18] c − [ ] c = [8] c

Thea bought:

Ethan bought 2 items.
He spent 14c.

[ ] c + [ ] c = [ ] c

Ethan bought:

Max had 20c.
His change was 15c.

[ ] c − [ ] c = [ ] c

Max bought:

Ruby bought 2 items.
She spent 17c.

[ ] c + [ ] c = [ ] c

Ruby bought:

Teacher's notes

Children complete the addition or subtraction problem to find out which item or items each character buys. They draw the item or items into the space underneath each one.

Date: ____________________

Pyramid puzzles

Write related addition and subtraction facts

Teacher's notes

Children use the numbers on each pyramid to write four related facts: two addition facts and two subtraction facts.

Date: ____________________

Add on 10, take off 10

Add and subtract 10 to or from a number

You will need:
- coloured pencils

1	2	3	4	5	6	7	8	9	10
11	12	13	14	15	16	17	18	19	20
21	22	23	24	25	26	27	28	29	30
31	32	33	34	35	36	37	38	39	40
41	42	43	44	45	46	47	48	49	50

3	+	10	=		18	−	10	=	
	+	10	=			−	10	=	
	+	10	=			−	10	=	
	+	10	=			−	10	=	
	+	10	=			−	10	=	

Teacher's notes

Referring to the 1–50 grid, children find each number with a square around it, and add 10 to the number, drawing a square around the answer in the same colour. They then complete each calculation as an addition fact in the boxes. Next, they look at each number that has been circled on the grid, and subtract 10 from the number, drawing a circle around the answer in the same colour. Finally, they complete each calculation as a subtraction fact.

Date: ____________________

2-D shape patterns

Complete 2-D shape patterns

You will need:
- coloured pencils

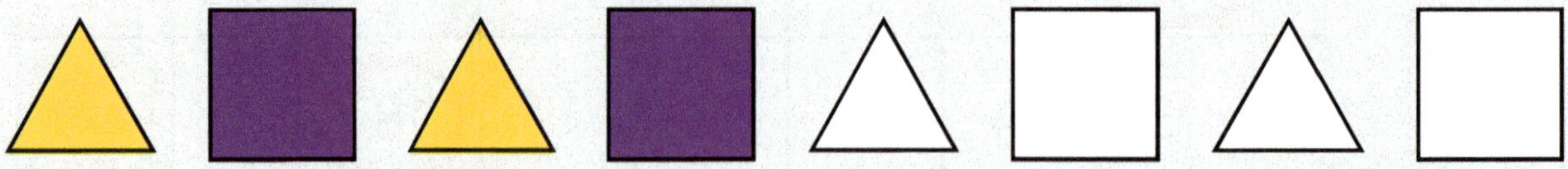

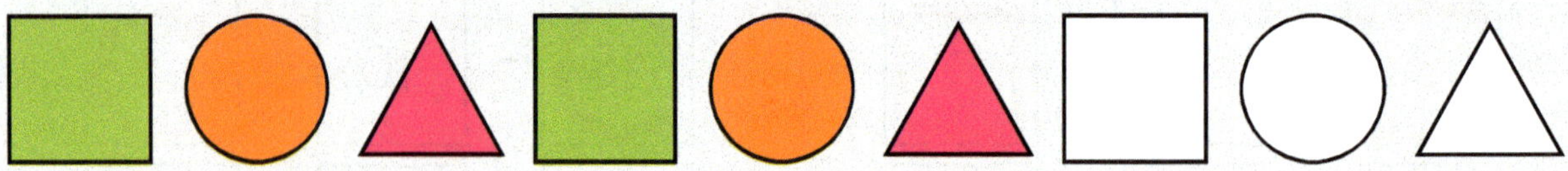

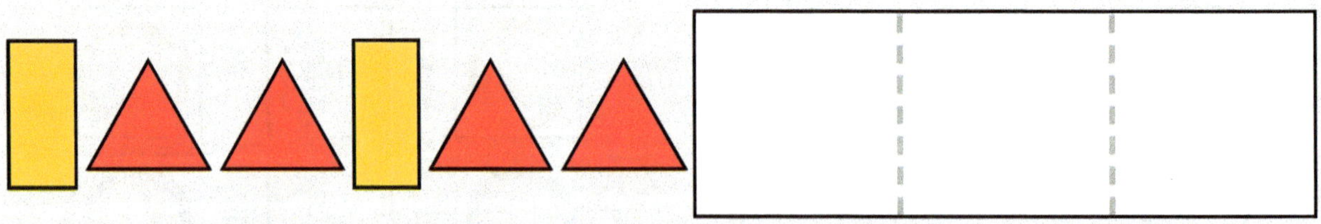

Teacher's notes

Children colour the shapes to continue the colour pattern. They then draw the shapes within the boxes to complete a pattern. Finally, they make up their own shape and colour pattern.

Date: ____________________

Name that 2-D shape

Name 2-D shapes

rectangle circle triangle square

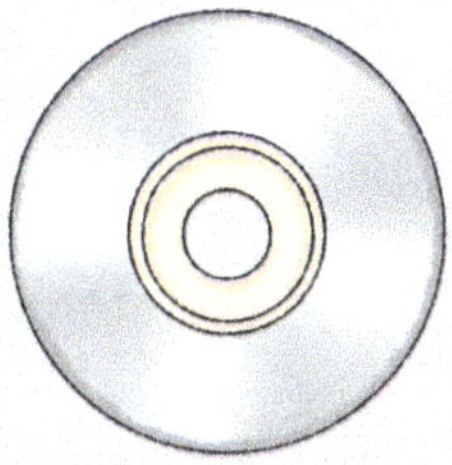

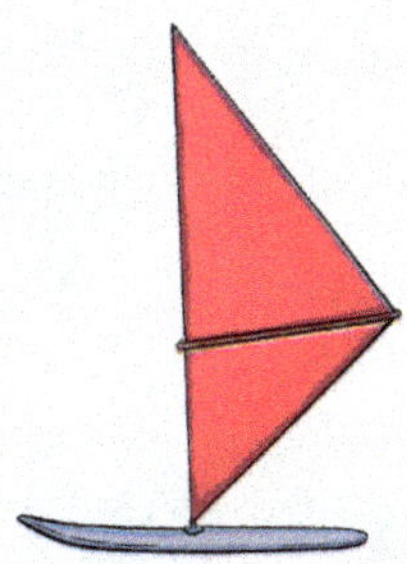

Teacher's notes

Children write the shape name for each object.

Date: ____________

3-D shape patterns and models

Make patterns and models using 3-D shapes

You will need:

- coloured pencils
- 3-D shapes: cuboids, cubes, pyramids, spheres, cylinders and cones
- camera

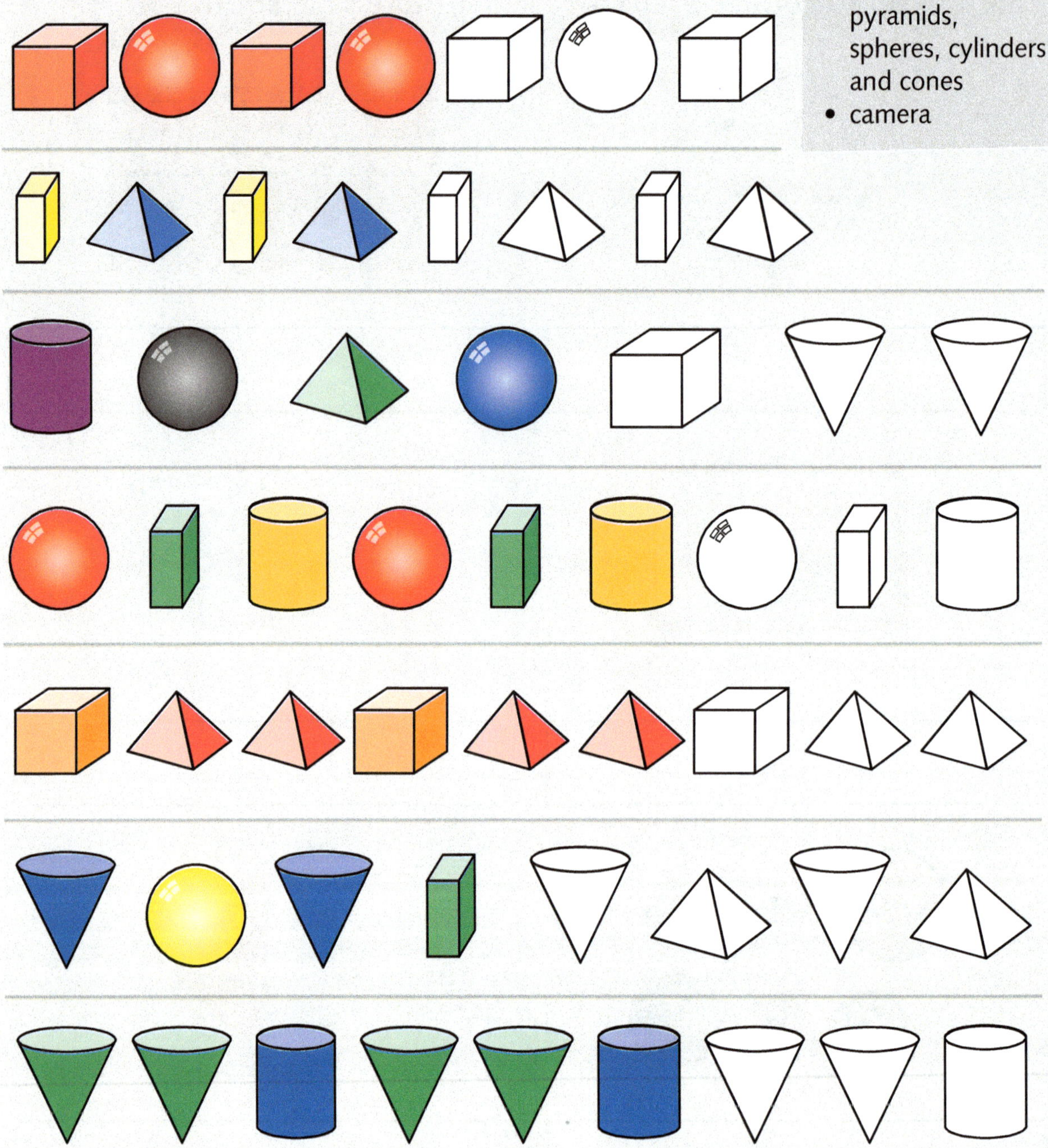

Teacher's notes

Children colour only the shapes that are part of a repeating pattern and leave the rows that aren't repeating patterns uncoloured. They then use cuboids, cubes, pyramids, spheres, cylinders and cones to build a model such as a castle or a train and take a photograph of the model.

Date: ____________________

Name that 3-D shape

Name 3-D shapes

cone cylinder sphere

pyramid cuboid cube

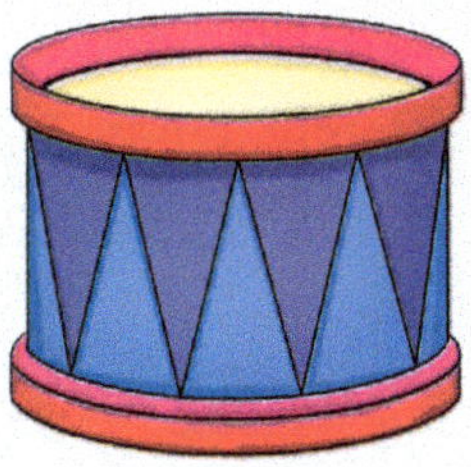

[ ]

[ ]

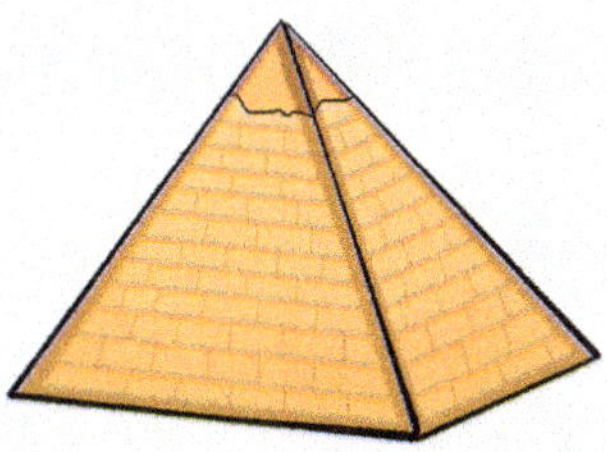

[ ]

[ ]

[ ]

[ ]

Teacher's notes

Children write the shape name for each object.

Date: ______________

Pirate hat doubles

Double numbers to 10

Teacher's notes

Children draw a line to match each pirate to the parrot that shows double the number on their hat.

Date: ____________________

Pirate halves

Find half of a number or set of objects

Half of 8 is ___.

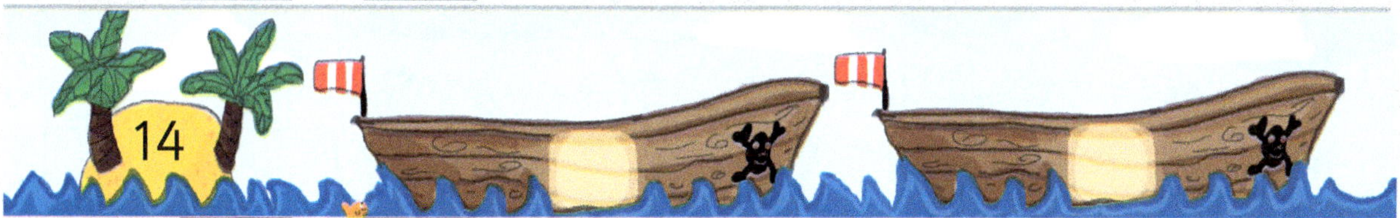

Half of ___ is ___.

Half of ___ is ___.

Half of ___ is ___.

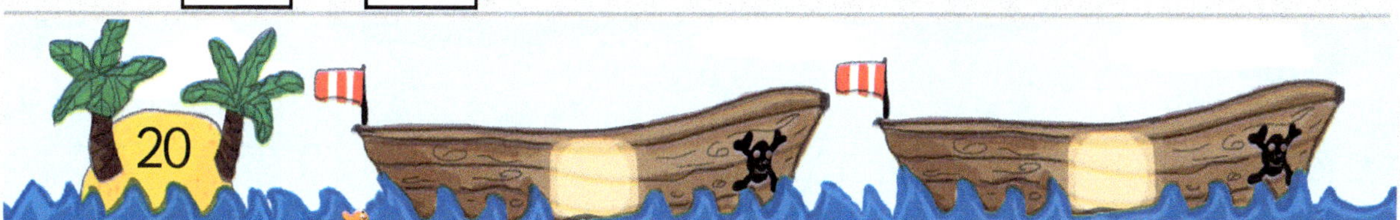

Half of ___ is ___.

Teacher's notes

Children look at the number on each island, which represents the number of pirates that need to go in the boats. Then they draw half the pirates in one boat and half in the other. Then they complete the sentence to find half of each number.

Date: ____________

Treasure troves

Find one quarter of a number or set of objects

One quarter of [12] is [ ].

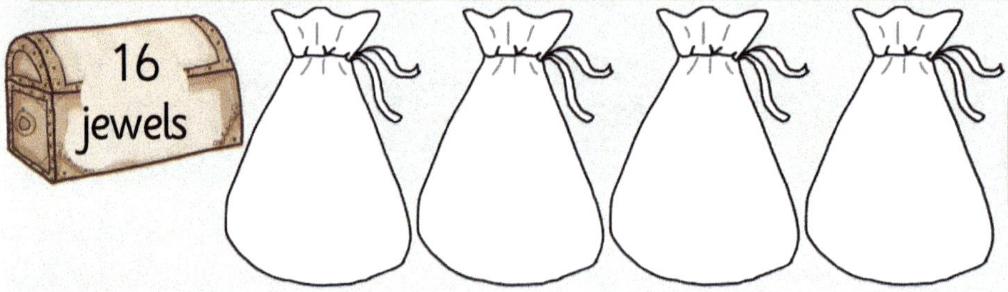

One quarter of [ ] is [ ].

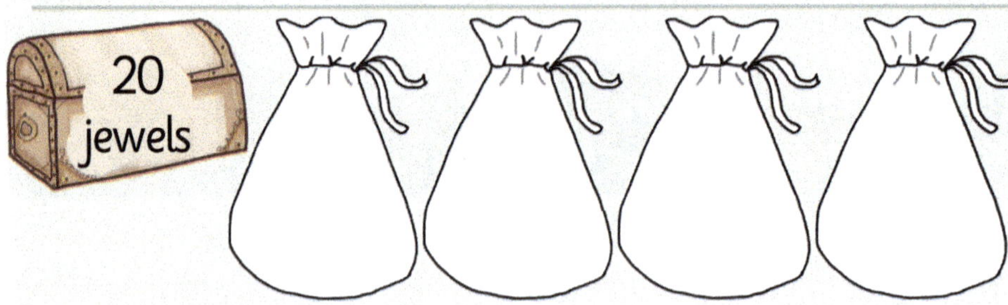

One quarter of [ ] is [ ].

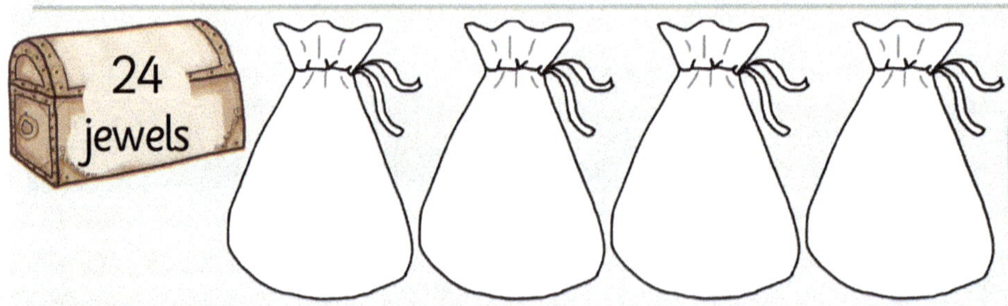

One quarter of [ ] is [ ]

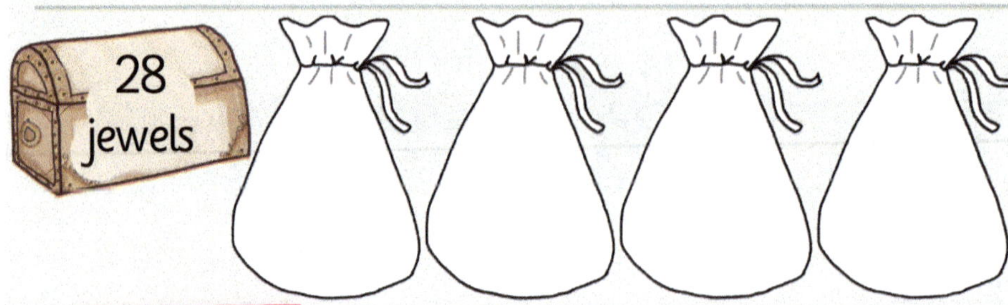

One quarter of [ ] is [ ].

Teacher's notes

Children look at the number of jewels in each treasure chest, and then share them equally between the four bags by drawing them in the spaces, to find one quarter. They then complete each sentence to show one quarter of each set of jewels.

Doubles, halves and quarters

Date: ____________

Find doubles, halves and quarters of numbers

Caie bought 2 fish stickers. Each one cost 7c. How much did he spend?

Ayesha had 8 charms on her bracelet. This was half of her charm collection. How many charms did she have altogether?

Laura had 12 sweets. This was double the number of sweets Amber had. How many did Amber have?

Cavan shared 16 biscuits into quarters. How many biscuits did he give to each friend?

Patrick had 20 cars. He gave half of his collection to Lee. How many did he give to Lee?

Ciara had 20 stickers. She gave one quarter of them to Isaac. How many stickers did she give to Isaac?

Teacher's notes

Children read each problem carefully and decide whether it is a double, halve or quarter problem. They then work out the answer, using the space underneath each problem to show their working out.

Cake quarters and halves

Find one half and one quarter of a shape

Date: ____________________

You will need:
- ruler
- coloured pencils

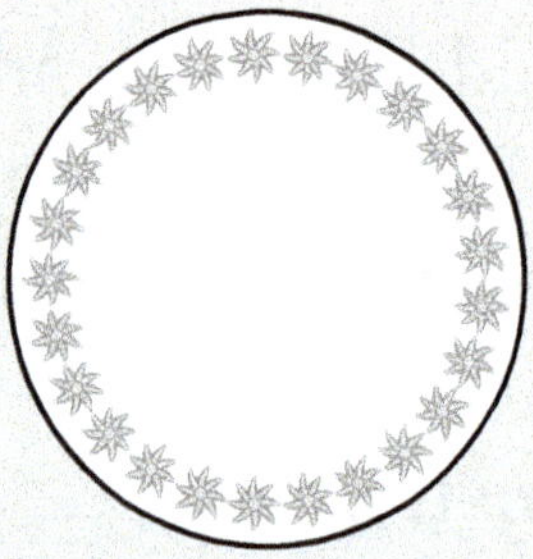

Divide the cake in half.
Colour one half.

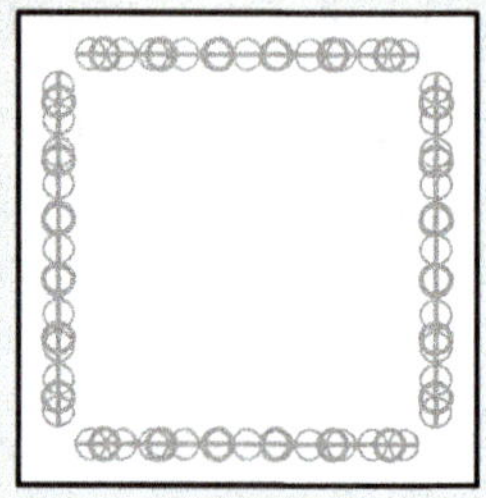

Divide the cake into quarters.
Colour one quarter.

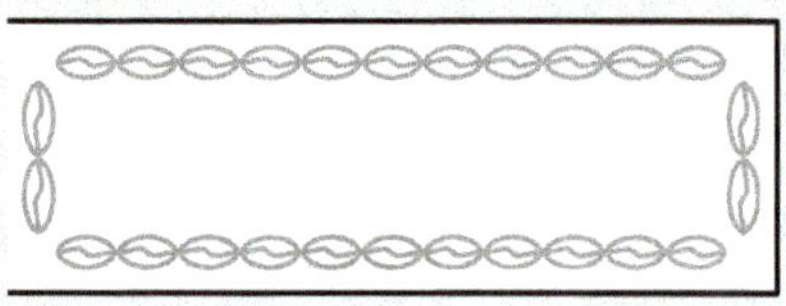

Divide the cake in half.
Colour one half.

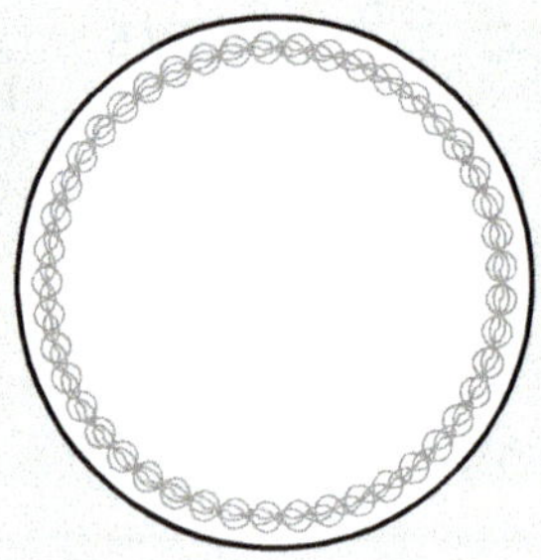

Divide the cake into quarters.
Colour one quarter.

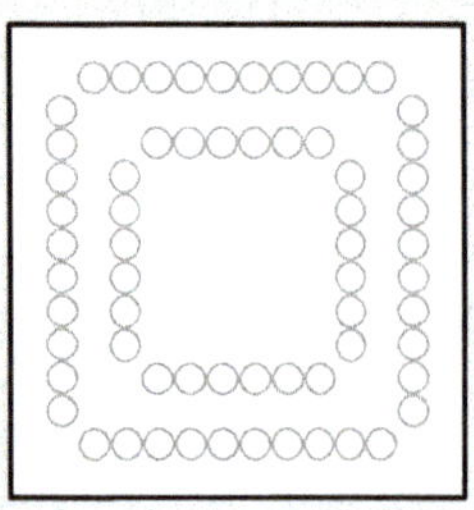

Divide the cake into quarters. Colour three quarters.

Divide the cake into quarters. Colour half of the cake.

Teacher's notes

Children follow the instructions to divide each cake into halves or quarters, drawing lines to divide each one. They then colour the fraction of the cake specified.

Halves and quarters questions

Date: ____________________

Find one half and one quarter of a set of objects

$\frac{1}{2}$ of ☐ is ☐.

$\frac{1}{4}$ of ☐ is ☐.

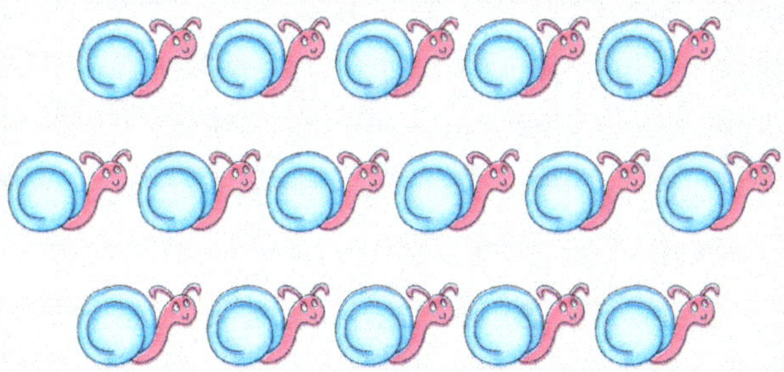

$\frac{1}{4}$ of ☐ is ☐.

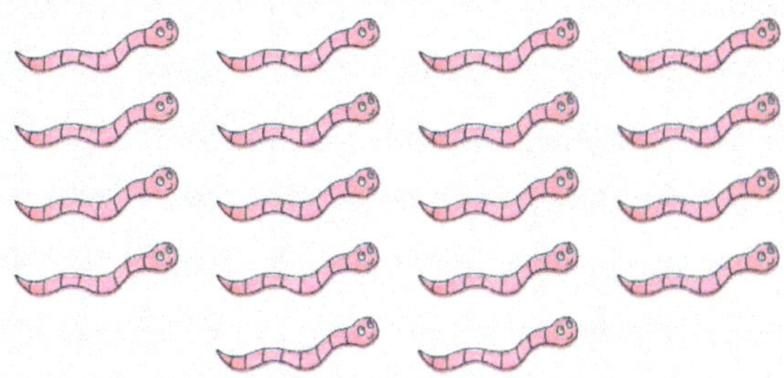

$\frac{1}{2}$ of ☐ is ☐.

$\frac{1}{2}$ of ☐ is ☐.

$\frac{1}{4}$ of ☐ is ☐.

Teacher's notes

Children count the number of minibeasts in each set, and find one half or one quarter of each set. They then complete the sentence underneath each set.

Flying carpet fractions

Recognise halves and quarters

Date: ____________________

You will need:
- coloured pencil

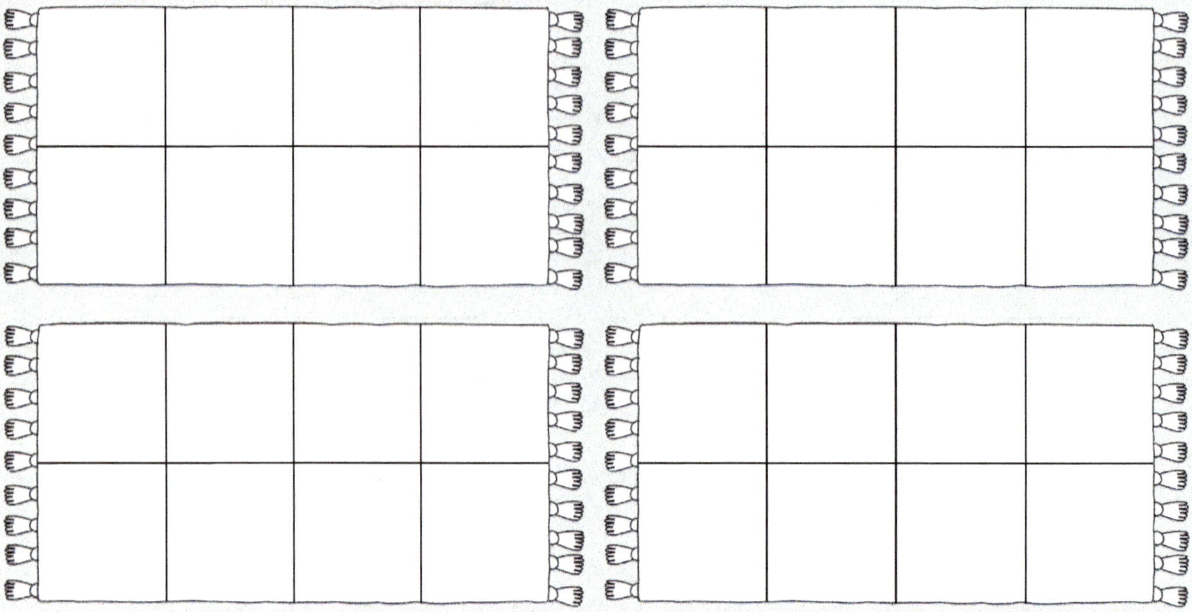

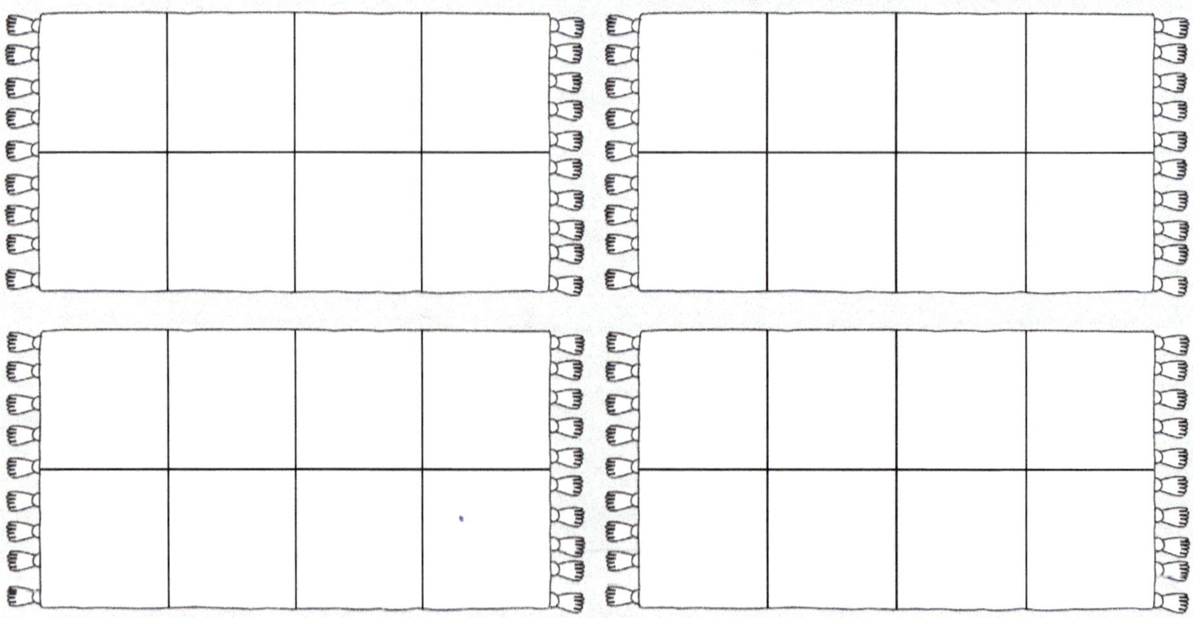

Teacher's notes

At the top of the page, using one colour for each carpet, children find different ways to colour half of each flying carpet. At the bottom of the page, again using one colour for each carpet, children find different ways to colour one quarter of each flying carpet.

Date: ____________________

Party fractions

Understand that fractions are related to grouping and sharing

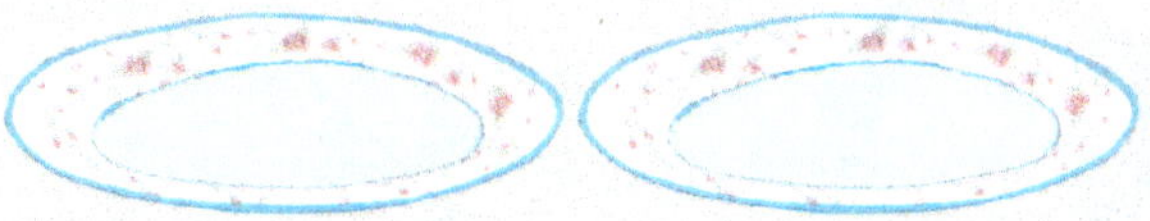

Half of ☐ is ☐.

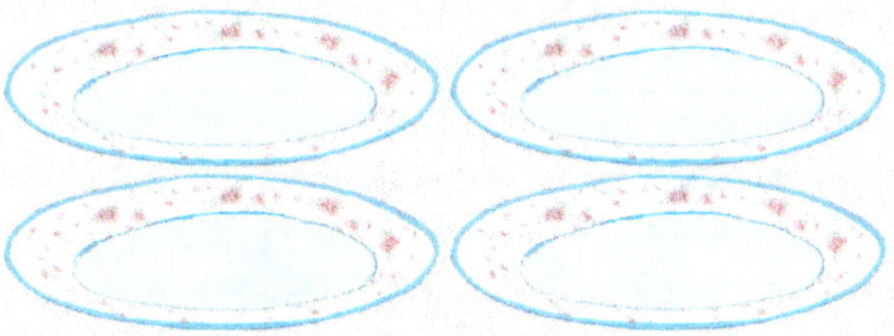

One quarter of ☐ is ☐.

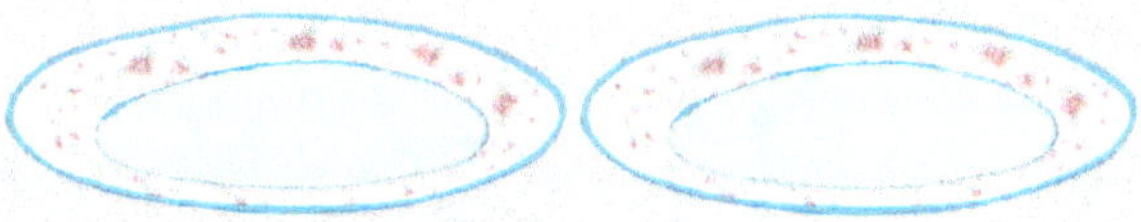

Half of ☐ is ☐.

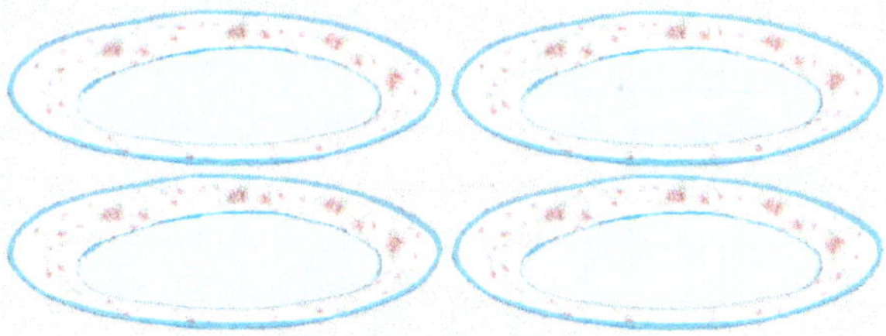

One quarter of ☐ is ☐.

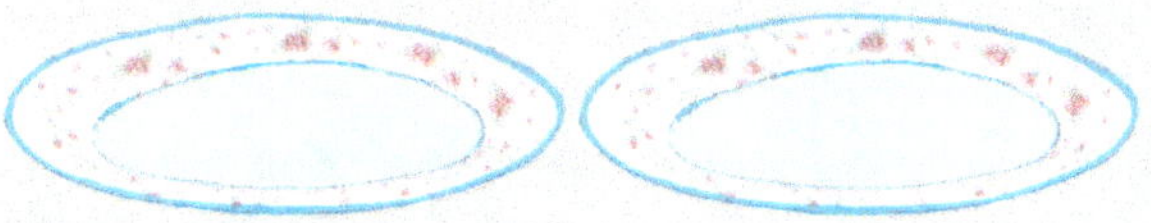

$\frac{1}{2}$ of ☐ is ☐.

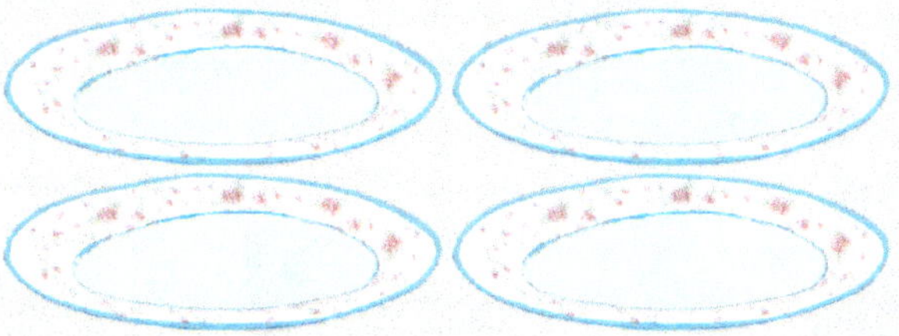

$\frac{1}{4}$ of ☐ is ☐.

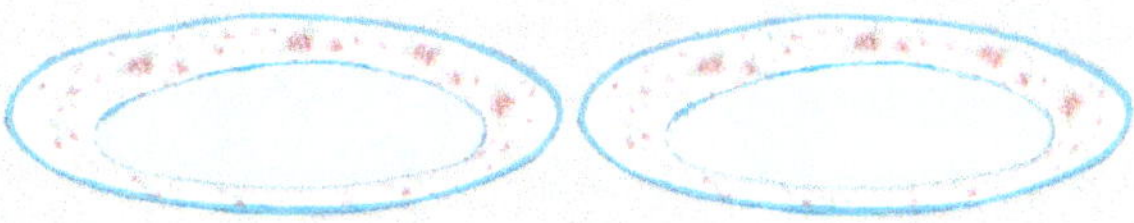

$\frac{1}{2}$ of ☐ is ☐.

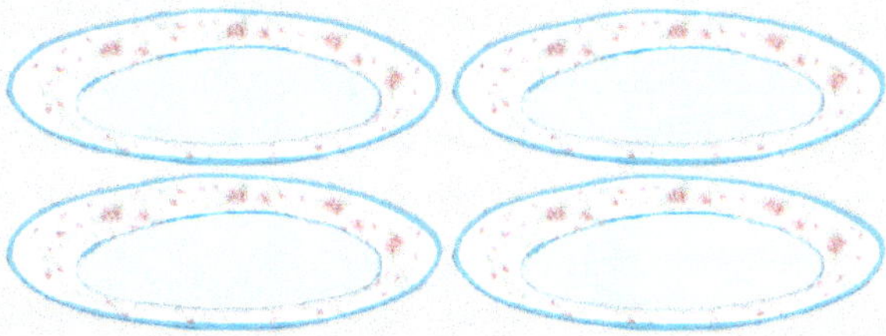

$\frac{1}{4}$ of ☐ is ☐.

Teacher's notes

Children count the total number of each item of party food. They then share this number equally between the two plates by drawing them onto the plates to find half, and then complete each sentence underneath. Next, they share the total number equally between four plates by drawing them onto the plates to find one quarter of each, completing each sentence underneath.

Date: ____________________

What time is it?

Read times on clocks and understand time intervals

$\frac{1}{2}$ hour later	$\frac{1}{2}$ hour earlier	1 hour later	1 hour earlier

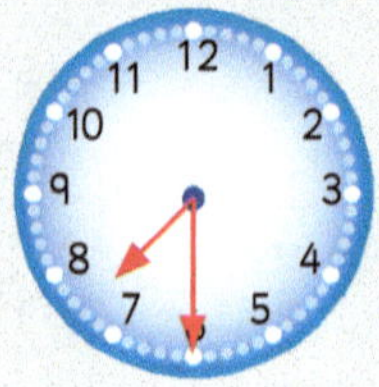

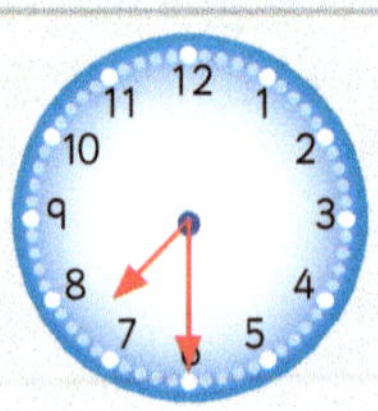

Teacher's notes

Children look at each clock and write the time (as an o'clock time). They then choose one of the vocabulary labels to write in the final box to describe the time interval between the two events shown.

Drawing hands

Date: ____________

Read and draw hands on clocks to show the time to the hour and half hour

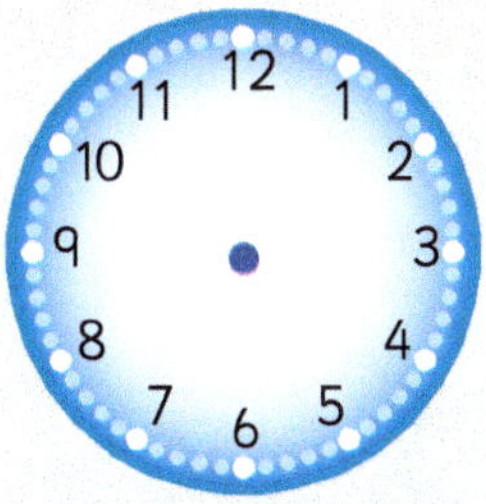 ← 1 hour earlier  1 hour later → 

 ← 1 hour earlier 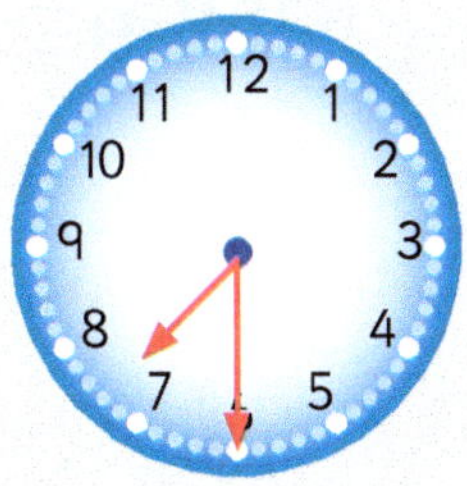 1 hour later → 

 ← 1 hour earlier 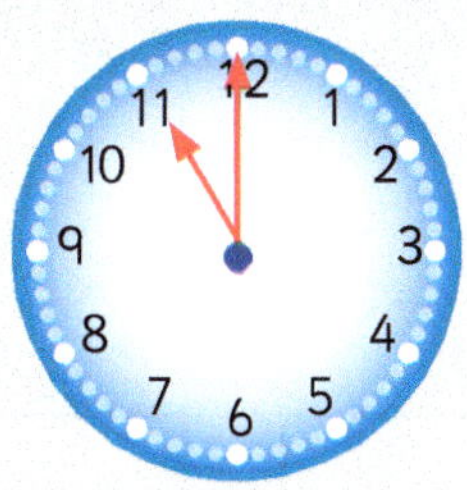 1 hour later → 

 ← 1 hour earlier 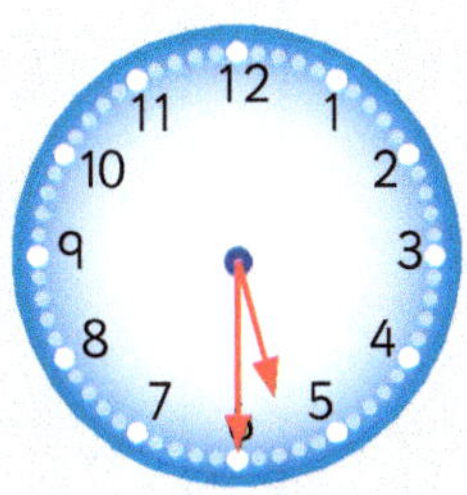 1 hour later → 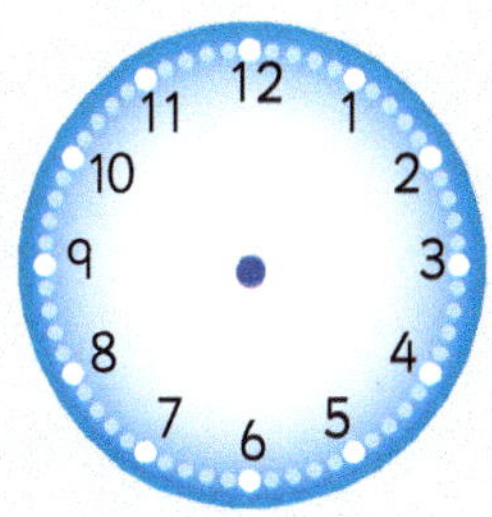

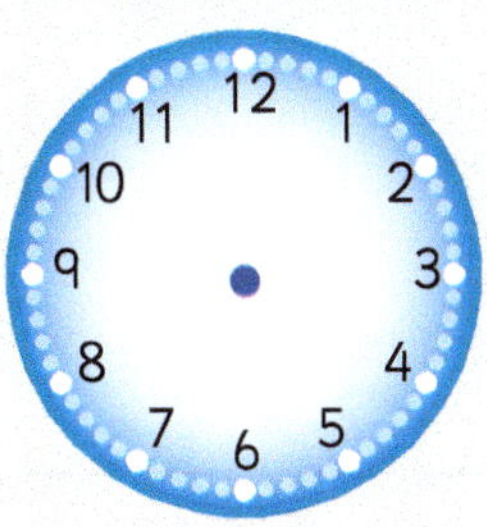 ← 1 hour earlier 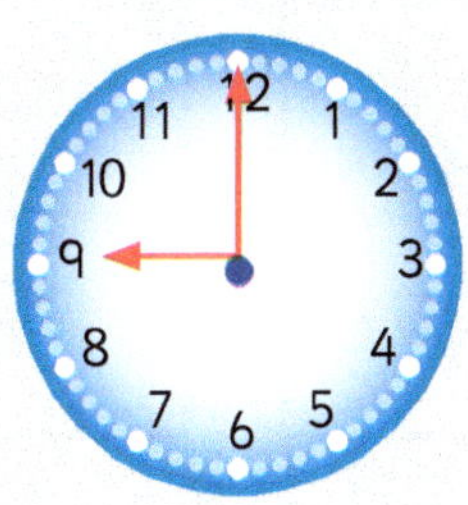 1 hour later → 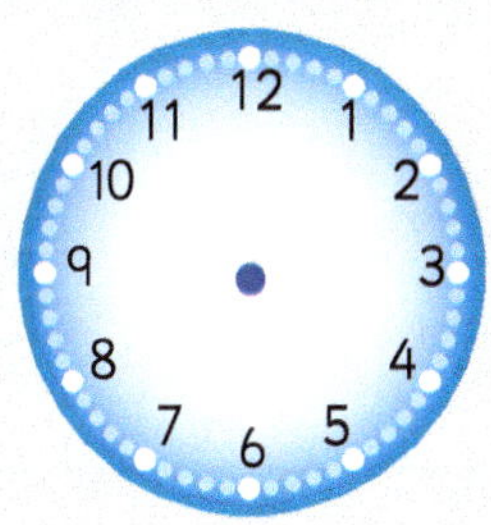

Teacher's notes

Children draw times on the clock faces to show the earlier or later times as shown on the arrows.

Date: ____________________

What can I do in 1 minute and 1 hour?

Begin to understand how long 1 minute and 1 hour are

minute

hour

About 1 minute	About 1 hour

Teacher's notes

Children look at each picture then draw a line to show whether the activity would last about 1 minute or 1 hour. They then draw something else that lasts about 1 minute and about 1 hour.

Date: ____________________

Journey times

Solve problems relating to time

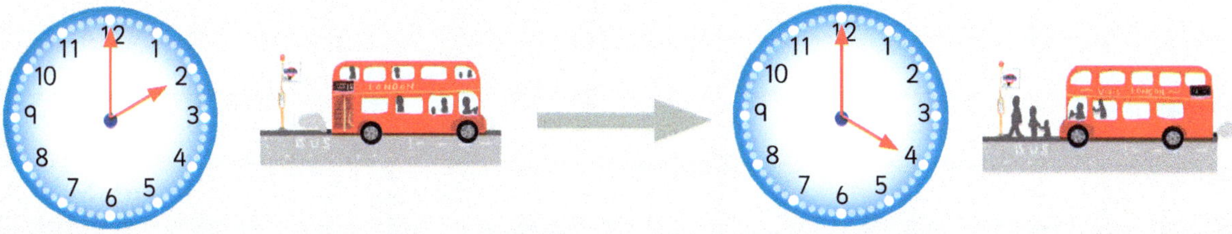

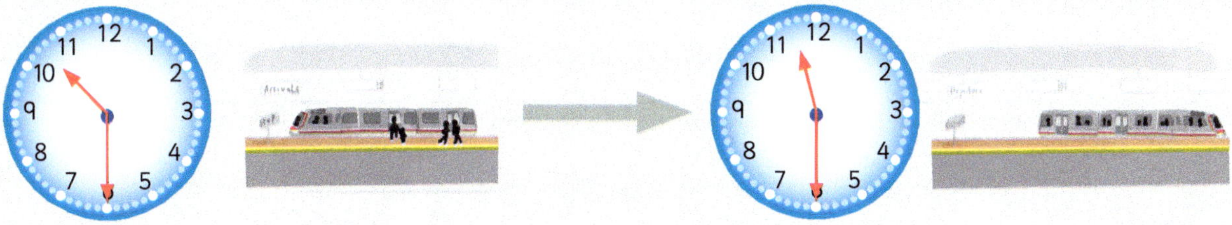

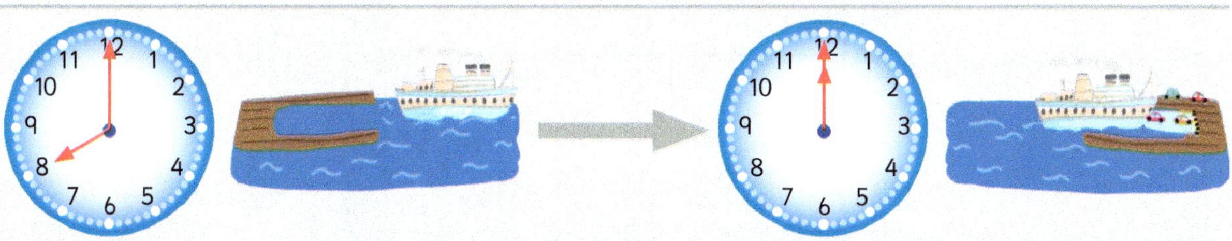

Teacher's notes

For each question, children look at the times shown on each clock and work out the difference in time between each journey. They write their answer in the box provided in hours and half hours, e.g. 1 and a half hours.

Maths facts

Number and place value

Numbers 0–20

0 1 2 3 4 5 6 7 8 9 10 11 12 13 14 15 16 17 18 19 20

Steps of 2

0 2 4 6 8 10 12 14 16 18 20 22 24

Steps of 5

0 5 10 15 20 25 30 35 40 45 50 55 60

Steps of 10

0 10 20 30 40 50 60 70 80 90 100

1–100 number square

1	2	3	4	5	6	7	8	9	10
11	12	13	14	15	16	17	18	19	20
21	22	23	24	25	26	27	28	29	30
31	32	33	34	35	36	37	38	39	40
41	42	43	44	45	46	47	48	49	50
51	52	53	54	55	56	57	58	59	60
61	62	63	64	65	66	67	68	69	70
71	72	73	74	75	76	77	78	79	80
81	82	83	84	85	86	87	88	89	90
91	92	93	94	95	96	97	98	99	100

Addition and subtraction

Number facts

+	0	1	2	3	4	5	6	7	8	9	10
0	0	1	2	3	4	5	6	7	8	9	10
1	1	2	3	4	5	6	7	8	9	10	11
2	2	3	4	5	6	7	8	9	10	11	12
3	3	4	5	6	7	8	9	10	11	12	13
4	4	5	6	7	8	9	10	11	12	13	14
5	5	6	7	8	9	10	11	12	13	14	15
6	6	7	8	9	10	11	12	13	14	15	16
7	7	8	9	10	11	12	13	14	15	16	17
8	8	9	10	11	12	13	14	15	16	17	18
9	9	10	11	12	13	14	15	16	17	18	19
10	10	11	12	13	14	15	16	17	18	19	20

+	11	12	13	14	15	16	17	18	19	20
0	11	12	13	14	15	16	17	18	19	20
1	12	13	14	15	16	17	18	19	20	
2	13	14	15	16	17	18	19	20		
3	14	15	16	17	18	19	20			
4	15	16	17	18	19	20				
5	16	17	18	19	20					
6	17	18	19	20						
7	18	19	20							
8	19	20								
9	20									

Measurement (time)

4 o'clock

$\frac{1}{2}$ past 8

Fractions

Half: $\frac{1}{2}$

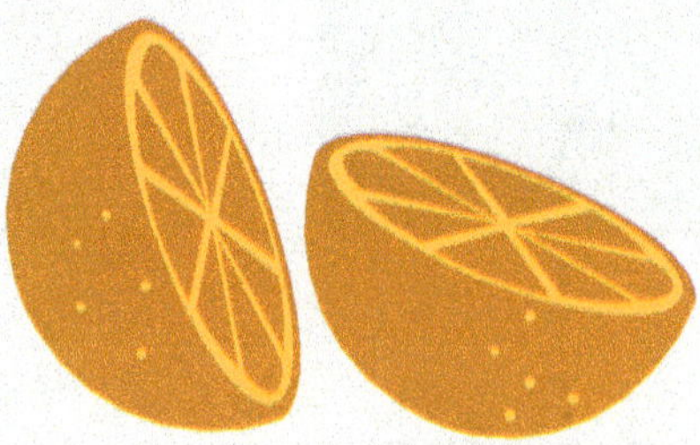

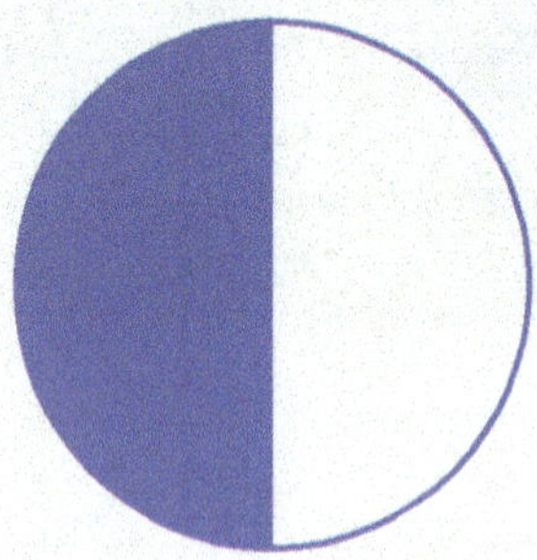

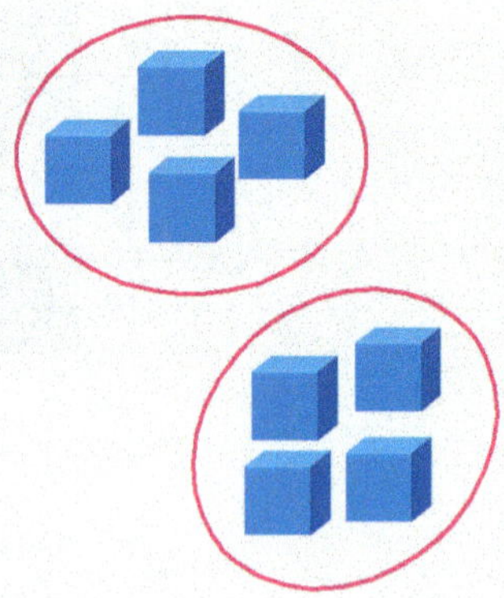

Quarter: $\frac{1}{4}$

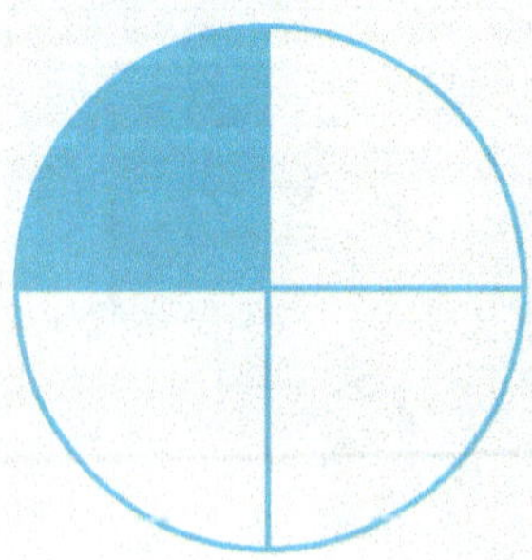

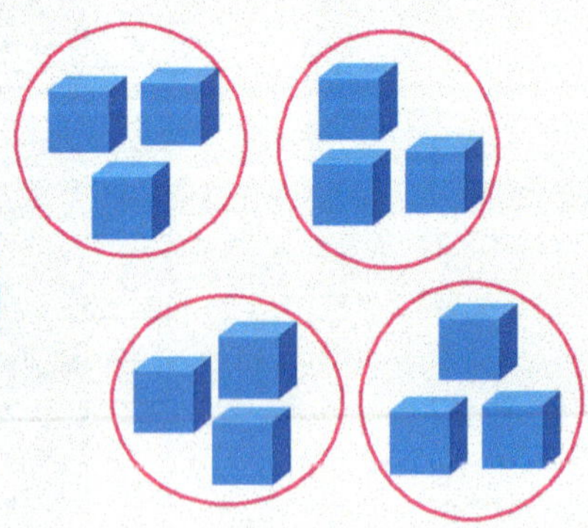

Properties of shape

2-D shapes

circle

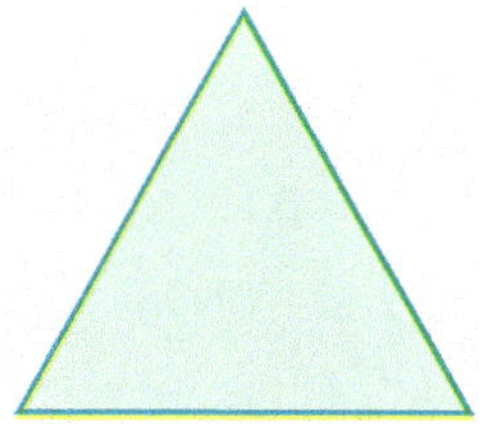
triangle

square

rectangle

3-D shapes

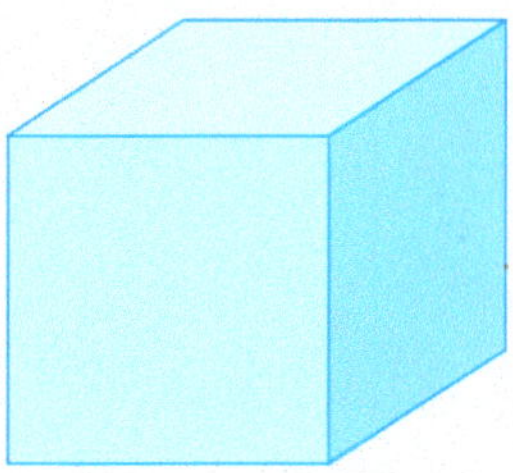
cube

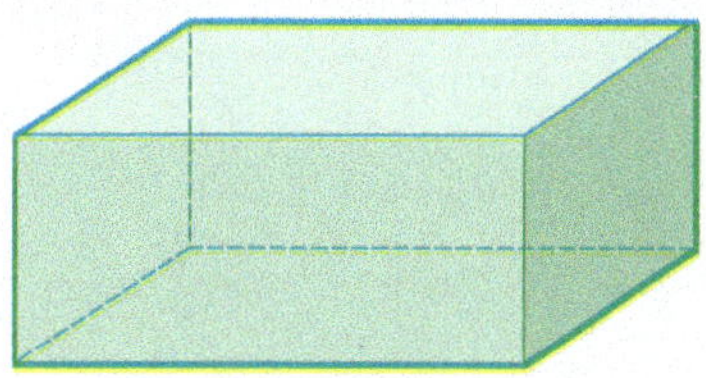
cuboid

cone

cylinder

sphere

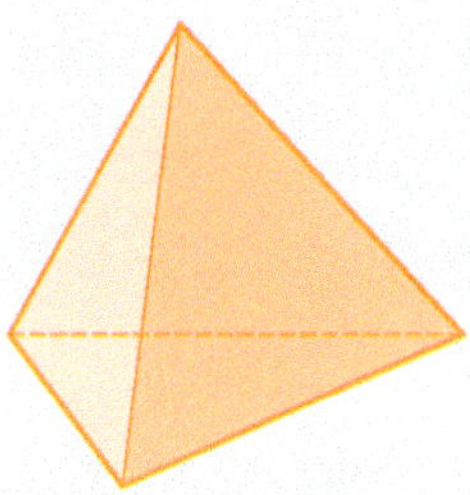
triangular-based pyramid

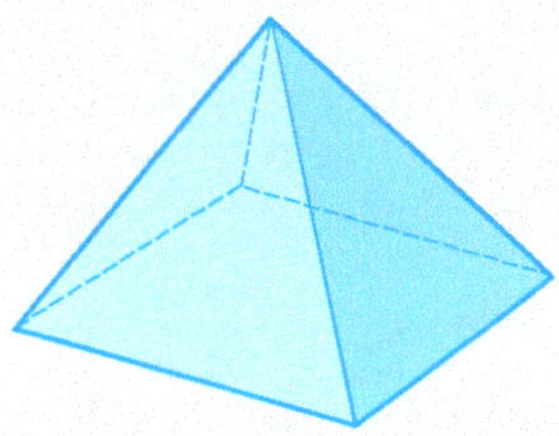
square-based pyramid